I0111015

BROKEN
TO BE
RESTORED

**Overcoming Failure and Defeat to
Live a Fully Restored Life**

Artnel L. Simon Jr.

TLZ Publishing
Kingston, Jamaica W.I.

Published by
TLZ Publishing
Kingston, Jamaica W.I.
www.TeddyAJones.com

Chantel Banbury, editor
chanban.cb@gmail.com

Khalid Johnson, Cover Designer
khalidjohnson267@gmail.com

Layout and eBook by
N.D. Author Services [NDAS]
www.NDAuthorServices.com

Table of Contents

Introduction

Broken to be Restored is a Christian-based book that sheds light on the journey of a young man encapsulated with his personal experiences. The purpose of this book is to provide motivation and hope to inspire persons who have been broken spiritually, mentally, emotionally or otherwise. It will provide encouragement to those experiencing 'brokenness' in any aspect of life.

This is an incredible book to empower you and help you move away from past torment. It is a fact that persons who experience massive suffering as they age, those memories often keep them enslaved. The brokenness you have encountered may have resulted in an increased level of distress, pain, stress, and desperate circumstances. Nevertheless after all that brokenness there is a plan for restoration. Each "suffering" God permits in your life can be turned around for His glory. God promises to remove the sins, and the impact of wrongdoing that has destroyed you.

This book is packed with biblical philosophy, encouragement and motivation that will keep you uplifted in the event that someone in your path is suffering heartache and needs restoration.

Furthermore, you will understand that being broken by God is a divine way so He can take you to a higher plane with Him. To be broken by God can advance you and lift you to a place where you can encounter another gift to be utilized and filled by Him. God will utilize these challenging times to fortify and set you up for what is coming. You are fortified for victory and your brokenness has the power to take you beyond limits.

Chapter 1:
Gracefully Broken

We are troubled on every side, yet not distressed; we are perplexed, but not in despair; persecuted, but not forsaken; cast down, but not destroyed (2 Corinthians 4:8-9).

Broken down in order to be lifted up. When you first hear the contradictory terms appear in conjunction, it causes you to ask the question: How can someone be broken down gracefully?

Being gracefully broken means surrendering everything, pouring out our hearts, all based on the knowledge that our brokenness has a purpose. The extremely powerful song "Gracefully Broken" by Matt Redman and Tasha Cobbs Leonard has truly inspired me. It is a beautiful song about surrender and how being gracefully broken actually helps us to become free. The bridge captures beautifully what being gracefully broken actually means:

God will break you to position you
Break you to promote you
And break you to put you in your right place
But when He breaks you He doesn't hurt you,
    He doesn't
When He breaks you He doesn't destroy you,
    He does it with grace.

I therefore trust that God utilizes our brokenness to make us more grounded. My favorite mantra is, "one will never know genuine euphoria without feeling torment." It is through our struggles and experiences that we turn to Him who is our tower of strength for assistance. When we fall on our knees, unfit to make another stride, that's when we are most grounded in Christ. In the event that life was perfect and without inconveniences, we would have no compelling reason to believe in Jesus, as we would be able to do it by ourselves. Our brokenness transforms us; it enables us to understand that without Christ, we are nothing. It is the point at which we understand that we don't need to deal with our burdens alone and that God has set us free.

The Lord is so deliberate with making us solid from our shortcomings. He needs us to depend on Him completely and not when we feel ready. The Lord's arrangement is deliberate, delightful, effortless... a move of trust, love and surrender is required. I never believed that being broken could be a gift but God has helped me see that my agony just allows me to adore Him all the more profoundly.

We live in a world where broken things are scorned and tossed out. Merchandise that do not meet the stipulated standards are rejected, and that includes individuals. In marriages, when couples separate, the inclination is to leave and discover another person as opposed to work at a compromise. The world is brimming with individuals who have broken hearts, broken spirits and broken connections.

"The Lord is close to the broken-hearted and saves those who are crushed in spirit" (Psalm 34:18). There is something about reaching a breaking point that causes us to seek the Lord more sincerely.

The Bible says that God breaks those who are proud and rebellious. The mighty Pharaoh hardened his heart and set himself against God. It was only a matter of time before God broke him and freed His people from bondage and shame. "I am the Lord your God, who brought you out of Egypt so that you would no longer be slaves to the Egyptians; I broke the bars of your yoke and enabled you to walk with heads held high" (Leviticus 26:13). God punishes all those who proudly resist Him. "My servants will sing out of the joy of their hearts, but you will cry out in anguish of heart and wail in brokenness of spirit" (Isaiah 65:14).

God has a very special plan and purpose for each of our lives, and He works relentlessly to cause that plan and purpose to come to pass. Let us look at the potter and the clay in Jeremiah 18:1-4:

The word which came to Jeremiah from the Lord, saying, Arise, and go down to the potter's house, and there I will cause thee to hear my words. Then I went down to the potter's house, and, behold, he wrought a work on the wheels. And the vessel that he made of clay was marred in the hand of the potter: so he made it again another vessel, as seemed good to the potter to make it.

Who is the potter in this story? It is God. Does God lack the ability to form a vessel? Did not the L ORD God form a man from the dust of the ground and breathed into his nostrils the breath of life, and the man became a living being? See Genesis 2:17. Therefore we can know for certain that the problem wasn't with the potter and his ability. That means that the problem must have been with the clay. For some reason the clay wouldn't cooperate that day.

Perhaps there were still some impurities in the clay that still needed to be removed. Or perhaps there were air bubbles that would cause the finished product to be weak. Maybe the clay was too wet or too dry. We don't know what the problem was; we only know that there was something wrong that would cause the finished product to be less than the potter's vision for it.

The potter could have thrown the clay away at this point. He could have said that this clay was completely useless and discarded it. But instead he chose to refine whatever was wrong with the clay and start again. There's a beautiful hymn about this passage titled "He Didn't Throw the Clay Away." The first verse says:

Empty and broken, I came back to Him

A vessel unworthy, so scarred from sin.
But He did not despair... He started over
   again
And I bless the day, He didn't throw the clay
   away.

At times, we find ourselves on the potter's wheel and we know why. But there will also be a time when we don't know why. As far as we can tell, we're doing everything we can to serve God and to do His will. But, without any warning or explanation, we feel the pressure of the potter's hand as He is remolding and remaking us. When this happens, the temptation is for us to become angry with God and perhaps question His wisdom and goodness.

There is an important verse of scripture found in the book of Isaiah that we need to plant deep within in our hearts. Isaiah 45:9 says "Woe to those who quarrel with their Maker... woe to the pot that contends with the potter and questions whether or not God knows what He is doing" (Author's translation).

It's hard when you find yourself being refashioned and you really don't know why. However, we must resist the temptation to become angry with God and question His judgment. Instead, we must submit our lives to our Maker and allow Him to perform His will.

God is the potter and we are the clay. Because we are clay, we won't always understand what God is doing. God says in His Word—

As the heavens are higher than the earth, So are my ways higher than your ways and my thoughts than your thoughts (Isaiah 55:9 NIV).

Just because we don't understand doesn't mean that there's not an explanation. It only means that we don't always understand the Creator. We cannot always see the areas in our lives that need improvement. We cannot always see what lies in the future. We cannot always understand how something bad today could turn out for good tomorrow. God is the potter and we are the clay. Therefore we must choose to trust in the goodness of God and seek His will as He reveals it.

We will not always understand what God is doing in our lives, nor why He is doing it. Sometimes the process will be very painful and confusing. But perhaps it is in those moments of pain and confusion that God is able to do some of His best work. Perhaps it is in those moments of brokenness that the Potter is able to gently fashion the vessel into something beautiful for His glory.

We are broken gracefully by our circumstances, we are re-established and spared. Indeed, it is excruciating. It may be the worst thing you've ever confronted, however, give me a chance to help you to remember Jeremiah 29:11: "For I know the plans I have for you," declares the Lord, "plans to prosper you and not to harm you, plans to give you hope and a future. Smoothly we were broken and nimbly we are being re-established, and we are given a chance to experience our lives to the magnificence of God, in light of the fact that by His beauty are we spared, mended, reclaimed and re-established.

Gracefully broken is to broken by God so He can take you to another dimension with Him, to be broken so God can advance you and place you in a place where you can encounter another gift, to be utilized and filled by Him.

At the point when God breaks you, he does it so impeccably that when amidst brokenness/the breaking, He discloses to you His beauty (support, corresponding power) is with you. At the point when God utilizes elegance to break you, it implies He is going to include support in your life. You are going to discover support in His eyes. Read 1 Samuel 2:26 and 1 Samuel 16:22.

When he breaks you, you begin getting affection, happiness and realizing that He never leaves you nor does He forsake you (Hebrews 13:5).

Even in the event that you've never given careful consideration to God, an extreme emergency has a method of swinging you to Him. You understand that except God comes through, you are not going to make it. Thus you shout out, "Goodness, God, help me!"

Some of you might be there this moment. It might be a medical issue; except God intercedes, there's no expectation. Maybe it's a genuine conjugal or family issue, a financial issue or an urgent requirement for work. It might be an individual issue, for example, forlornness, blame, outrage, harshness, or uneasiness. It could be some life-ruling sin, for example, liquor, medications, sex entertainment, or betting. In any case, whatever the issue, you realize that you require God, and you're calling out to Him for help.

Numerous individuals don't see the need to trust in Christ as their Savior since they hold tight to their faith in their very own decency. Their pride blinds them to their incredible need before God.

"Come let us return to the Lord; for He has torn us, that He may heal us; He has struck us down, and He will bind us up" (Hosea 6:1). We don't normally think of God as one who destroys or tears down. We don't think the Lord would strike us down. But Hosea says otherwise and other Scriptures support the idea.

Hosea recognized that God can and will bring us down before building us up. It is often in the depths of our despair that we come to know God. Only when there is nothing left do we really see His love for us. Even Paul had trouble understanding this idea until he had begged for deliverance from some unknown "thorn in the flesh" (2 Corinthians 12:1-10). His conclusion was in verses 9-10:

> I will boast all the more gladly of my weaknesses, so that the power of Christ may rest upon me. For the sake of Christ, then, I am content with weaknesses, insults, hardships, persecutions, and calamities. For when I am weak, then I am strong.

Chapter 2:
Jesus was Broken

Jesus suffered physically. The Romans' method of execution was one of the must inhumane way to take a human's life. The beating with the cat o-nine tails just about ended His life.

Jesus suffered emotionally. Never has anyone been so taunted, condemned, wrongly charged and neglected as the Savior. Those nearest to Him fled at a minute when He required them the most. John, Mary His mother and a couple of ladies were there until the end.

Jesus suffered spiritually. One will never completely grasp what it is like for heavenly nature to go up against fragile human living creatures and face every one of the allurements the demon laid before Him. However, after the physical and wholehearted misery, He bore the burdens of humanity's sin forever. To imagine that one would endure disgrace and blame over our transgression, yet He bore that for all.

Through everything, Jesus could state on the cross, "Father, forgive them; for they know not what they do." This was directed to the same persons who put a crown of thorn on His head and took a stick and beat His head taunting saying, "Let us know, prophet, who hit you." Cruelly forced the crown of thorn into His skull causing such torment and swelling that His face wound up unrecognizable (Isaiah 52:14). The wrinkles upon His face from the torment-ing (Psalm 22), the clear dejection that caused such pressure that He sweat blood; and through this, nonetheless, He had the compas-sion to state, 'I forgive you'.

From the feeling of the Last Supper one can picture that Jesus experienced both happiness and impactful distress at the trials He would face, the betrayal from Judas and the disap-pearing and coming suffering of the followers.

The distress He encountered in the Garden of Gethsemane, knowing from practical and His Divine understanding of the terrors of cru-cifixion, He pleaded, alone, uncomforted by His followers.

Jesus sweats blood (Luke 22:44), an uncommon and difficult condition called hematidrosis that happens amid times of extreme pressure/mental torment, leaving the skin incredibly delicate. At this state dehydration has started.

Aside from encountering the disappointment of His disciples in the Garden, Jesus encountered the betrayal from Judas, who cleverly sold out Him with a kiss (Luke 22:48) and the brutality from Peter (Luke 22:51). Foreseeing that Peter will deny Him, Jesus at that point saw Peter's denial (Luke 22:61).

From the Last Supper, Jesus didn't get any food, water or rest during a period of pressure and physical struggle. He was forced to walk for more than 2 miles as He walked around the Jewish authority, Pilate and Herod.

There were a few occasions where Jesus was hit in the face and head (Matthew 26:67 27:30) causing wounding and swelling. His nose was battered and swollen. The devastating (Matthew 27:26) tear in His body went close to his bones, leaving more than 120 injuries over His back, sides, legs and arms which overflowed with blood. The nail-like thorns penetrated the skin in many spots and maybe the skull, causing unbelievable torment and loss of blood (Matthew 27:29).

Jesus bore the cross with assistance from Simon of Cyrene (John 19:17) a distance of nearly ½ mile. The cross was weighty (100-200 pounds) wounding His shoulders. He fell many times scratching the skin off His knees. Weakened, He was nailed to the cross with nails that were driven through His hands (palms) and feet (John 25:20). The nerve thickness made these injuries especially unbearable and there was a huge loss of blood.

For three extended periods of time, His numerous injuries hurt. He attempted to lessen the burning nerve torment and tearing tissue by nails. His shoulders hurt as the joints are pulled. He was thirsty because of absence of water and lack of hydration from loss of blood and perspiring. His tormenting reasons for death by a mix of loss of blood, shock and suffocation.

Chapter 3:
God Has to Break You
to Make You

Once in a while God breaks us in the most badly arranged way. He will uncover the issues in our lives that are left unsolved in a sudden time and place, until we understand we can trick others yet we can never trick Him and even ourselves.

God's greatest leaders have always been broken before they could be used. Noah preached for 120 years and labored over a boat for many years. Abraham wandered like a nomad; Moses fled the luxury of Egypt to tend cattle; and even Jesus suffered in the wilderness. In fact, the Bible says Jesus "emptied Himself" (Philippians 2:7) so that He could redeem mankind.

You see lying wounded Abraham and he even had his better half lie and state she was not his wife, but the Lord revealed to Abraham I need to utilize you. Walk before me and be Holy. The Lord utilized him, blessed him and made him a great nation. Murder wounded Moses. But the Lord utilized him to lead his kin out of subjugation. Uncertainty wounded Gideon. He needed the Lord to give him suggestions and pondered his capacity. However, that did not prevent the Lord from utilizing him.

Peter turned on the Lord. However the Lord still utilized him to lecture the primary message upon the arrival of Pentecost. Paul was wounded by the wrongdoing of persecution, yet the Lord still utilized him. We don't need to remain in sacred writing; persons are wounded by infidelity. In any case, the Lord can utilize you. If you're wounded by any addiction or sinfulness the Lord can still use you. In the event that you're unfaithful, that is a wound.

Youthful people offending your folks, that is a wound. Cutting up and being rebellious, that is a wound. Whatever your wound is, God still wants to and is able to utilize you. You have the chance to go before the Lord, and say, "Lord against thee and thee alone have I sinned. Cleanse me with hyssops; wash me and I will be more white than snow. Create within me a clean heart and renew a right spirit within me" (Psalm 51 v. 4, 7, 10).

What's more, you can rest assured that God stands by His word. For He says if any man comes to me, I will not cast him out. God is concerned about your wounds. In any case, you got the opportunity to take it to the Lord in prayer.

As a defense mechanism, many of us have gotten so good at hiding our true feelings. We try to cover the torment we feel behind our smiles, and even though we are so good to make persons accept we're fine, we can never trick the One who made us and the One who cherishes us to send His only son.

In the Bible, God broke those who He wanted to use, and they became great and mighty men for Him.

Before Abraham became the father of many nations, he and Sarah were childless.

Before Jacob could be blessed, he was wounded by an angel in a wrestling match.

Before Joseph ruled Egypt, he was thrown into a pit, sold into slavery, and falsely imprisoned.

Before Job's estate was doubled, he lost everything he had, including his family, his fortune, and his future.

Before Moses became the great deliverer, he lost his position, his possessions, and his popularity.

Before Joshua conquered the Promised Land, he went through the wilderness.

Before Samson crushed the Philistines, he was blinded, and bound.

Before David became king, he was belittled by his family ridiculed by his foes, and rejected by his friends.

Before Daniel could be used, he had to spend the night in the lion's den.

Before Hosea became a powerful spokesman for God, his wife betrayed him, which broke him.

Before Peter preached 3,000 souls into the kingdom, he denied his Savior three times and went out and wept bitterly.

Before Paul brought the gospel to the Gentiles, he was blinded on the Damascus road.

Try not to allow Satan to deny you of your motivation, by telling you that you are nothing more than a bad memory to God.

Let's take a look at the woman with the issue of blood, she was wounded by depression and sickness, and, the Lord healed her. The blind man by the roadside was wounded, the Lord made him new and the Bible says he celebrated God. The Samaritan woman at the well was suffering; the Lord still settled her and utilized her. She became an evangelist in her town.

God realizes how you've been imploring and wrestling against daily temptation and He sees that you are nearly consumed. God knows sometimes as humans we are going to fall, yet God still wants to utilize us.

There is promise for you, you may have been running into barriers and getting all beat up however God wants to recuperate you. Medications, lying and slandering may have wounded you, yet still God wants to mend you.

Through the years, God has repaired many wounded persons and after that utilized them for His glory. Also, the Holy Book says He is the same God yesterday, today and forever more.

He will take us back to the past to recall the reasons for our feelings of anguish and tears; we can attempt to escape however we can never flee from the accounts and recollections that even up to this point plague us.

He will permit the second thoughts that eat at us and the distresses that expend us to assume control and have an enormous effect in our lives until the point that it fills its need.

BROKEN TO BE RESTORED

Attempt as we may, concealing and fleeing from those things and even 'He realizes when to shake our confidence and disclose the weights and abundant things we're conveying.

Our God is a God of surprises and frequently He will daze us with unexpected return of individuals whom we thought had been a distant memory from our circle. They might be messengers with words we never realized we'd at present have the capacity to hear, with circumstances we aren't prepared to confront, with confused things we are hesitant to acknowledge.

It may be difficult to understand why we have to face such awful experiences and even return to that bitter part of our lives. But, for what reason? Wouldn't we be able to simply proceed like nothing happened and carry on with a life free of stresses?

Indeed, life doesn't work that way. God doesn't work that path either; rather we need to confront the uncertain issues in our lives to prepare for the gift He is going to give. We should lower ourselves to surrender to Him the weights and baggage we've been holding so His delight can fill us. Let the distress and lament that visits us be a notification that He will be with all of us all through, and give this brokenness to Him as an accommodation that we are only pieces that must be settled by Him.

We have a decent Father above and simply like a biological dad is on Earth, He wants what's best for us. God wants to ensure that His kids will never get lost or tired while battling the fights that are in front of them and that regardless of what the circumstance might be, He will be clear in their lives.

So don't get confounded or shocked when the business of the past that we made a decent attempt to cover where it counts all of a sudden showed up once more, notwithstanding when we thought we were fine. Maybe God is genuinely moving in us and He's utilizing every one of those things to begin changing our broken lives and transform it into extraordinary and delightful ones.

Chapter 4: Misconceptions of Brokenness

Brokenness comes in several ways. Commonly it originates from a feeling of individual disappointment, genuine or anticipated. For some it maybe a broken marriage, the passing of a friend or family member, a failed activity or ruined accounts. For others the word cancer will prompt brokenness; whatever it is, the source of the circumstance isn't as important as our reaction to it. Despite the fact that the conditions might be dire, the perfect objective is to take lemons and make lemonade to use to our advantage our setbacks turning them into more significant things of God.

It is imperative for all of us to understand what brokenness isn't. Brokenness isn't just affliction. Enduring is a more extensive classi-fication than brokenness. All dads are con-sidered men yet not all men are fathers. In a similar way almost all brokenness has an en-during part to it yet not all enduring is broken-ness. Brokenness isn't repentance. You may in reality need to say I am sorry yet not all broken-ness requires repentance. It is that sort of brokenness that needs to be investigated. Also, it may not by any stretch of the imagination be brokenness. Notwithstanding, it feels so much like brokenness and looks so much like broken-ness that the condition is marked as broken-ness. It is expected that once one understand brokenness that does not require repentance then you will know where you are at and have the capability to deal with all brokenness.

Chapter 5:
Brokenness Reveals the
Power of the Flesh

Sin is a denominator in Christianity, but at the same time it's that negative word nobody likes to discuss. We would like to believe that individuals are fundamentally great. In any case, Christianity asserts that transgression has a noose on everyone. Before we lose trace of what's most important, how about we pause for a minute to characterize sin.

Sin includes any deviation from God's ideal standard of blessedness. This can be the consequence of our musings, our conduct or what we speak. Christ accentuated the significance of being inside good, not simply remotely moral. That is the reason He given His followers precedence, for example, "But I tell you that anyone who looks at a woman lustfully has already committed adultery with her in his heart" (Matthew 5:28).

Our evil conduct hurts others, hurts us and, more importantly, is an attack against the blessed God. This isn't God's method for removing all the enjoyment from life. Or maybe, in the event that we were intended to work best a specific way—living in amicability with God—at that point the best thing for us is to re-establish our broken association with God and appreciate life inside the parameters He has built up.

Because of transgression, we dismiss God and rather place ourselves in His place. This implies sin isn't just the reality of our division from God, but includes our stiff-necked non-compliance.

Be that as it may, what is the degree of wrongdoing? As indicated by the Bible, sin is all inclusive. All in all we are fallen and corrupt, Paul clarified, "As it is written: 'There is no one righteous, not even one; there is no one who understands; there is no one who seeks God. All have turned away, they have together become worthless; there is no one who does good, not even one." (Romans 3:10-12 NIV).

In particular, how frequently do you contemplate internally, personally pulled into your own liberalities—that you have put Christ Jesus to an open disgrace, in your wrongdoings, killing him over and over in your souls and minds and in the event that you should fall far from the Word of God, Christ Jesus, do you want to re-charge yourselves again unto contrition" (Hebrews 6:6, KJV).

Chapter 6:
Brokenness Reveals
the Power of God

Brokenness is a condition which God enables to test our lives to the point that we should absolutely rely upon him. From both experience and perception, it appears that the more significant God's plans are for an individual, the more evident the brokenness He requires.

The life of the witness Paul reflects both extraordinary power and incredible brokenness; yet, in contrast to the greater part of us, Paul never thought about his own conditions as discipline, he considered it to be a calling of administration to Christ.

At different occasions, God utilizes brokenness to get the individuals who definitely know him, to relinquish whatever keeps them from encountering him completely. In either case, brokenness implies perceiving that what we have isn't sufficient!!

In God's wisdom, He realizes what it takes to keep us in line with his direction, so He allows difficulties in our lives that will break our will and keep us dependent on him. James 1:2-3, "Consider it all joy, my brethren, when you encounter various trials, knowing that the testing of your faith produces endurance."

Now let me make this very clear: the word "brokenness" never appears in the scriptures, yet we know by inference that it is one of the most important concepts to the Christian life. Brokenness is expressed in 2 Corinthians 12:9 when Paul writes, "My grace is sufficient for you, for my strength is made perfect in weakness. Therefore most gladly I will rather boast in my infirmities, that the power of Christ may rest upon me."

Brokenness is a state of mind, whereby we recognize our personal weaknesses and limitations before God, and surrender to His will. Now please don't miss this: "total surrender" is the starting point of brokenness!

Your trials are a heartfelt invitation from God that ensures His closeness, and His active hand in your daily life and then His ministry will be magnified through you.

That is why Gideon needed only 300 men to rout an army of thousands.

That is why Moses, with his hands out-stretched to the Lord, in the presence of his enemies, was able to cause the defeat of that enemy and the parting of an entire sea.

That is why a small boy named David was able to kill a lion, a bear and a giant.

That is why David's three mighty men were able to penetrate the camp of the enemy.

That is why Joseph was elevated from the depths of a prison to the rank of second in command in Egypt.

That is why Jehoshaphat needed only a handful of worshippers to defeat an army of 100,000 men. And that is why Jesus needed only 12 men to turn the world up-side-down.

There is a confusing expression all through the Bible that says brokenness is quality, but in what way could this possibly be true? In what manner can brokenness be quality? At the point when an individual is broken, they are frequently baffled and harmed past articulation. However, to utilize people to their fullest degree, the Master needs to break His people so they have another sort of solidarity that isn't human in cause.

We ought to never fear brokenness! For some it takes a broken marriage, the passing of a friend or family member, a failed activity, or bankruptcy. God can utilize any of these scenes to tame our spirits, however the source isn't so critical as how we react to it.

Have you ever been at a point in life where it seemed as if you had been gifted with the luck of the Irish? Everything is going right and you feel on top of the world, then out of nowhere the walls of success and accomplishments just begin to tumble down?

Just before a 'jump' forward in your life, things will frequently separate.

Try not to be weakened in the event that you may experience a troublesome time or things look inverse than you anticipated. In spite of the fact that it isn't God's will for us, usually to encounter breakdowns before getting a re-markable forward movement in your life. There are numerous precedents all through the Bible where things looked inverse before a turn-around.

You may have experienced being very near to an achievement perhaps for as far back as couple of years, then things begin to occur, or start to change, and after that it appears to decrease and die down. These are given to us as stores to what is coming. There is increase on its way, regardless of whether it is steadily littler or in various parts of our lives than we have expected to see. We are being tested by the way we think and view circumstances. God is utilizing these attempting times to fortify and set you up for what is coming.

"I think about that our present sufferings are not worth contrasting and the brilliance that will be uncovered in us" (Romans 8:18).

It's not difficult to see that there is brokenness all over the place, surrounding us. Broken connections, broken hearts, broken bodies, broken social dimensions, and broken power systems. There is actually no domain or territory of humankind perfect by brokenness. Brokenness is a truth of the universe we live in, and a truth of our identity.

Before we can start to re-establish our relationship with God, we have to understand that this relationship is broken regardless and why that is the situation. The relationship is broken not in view of anything God has done, but rather on account of what we have done. We have gotten some distance from God's measures and made our very own way.

Chapter 7:
Your Past is Your Past

The past is the past. There's no use in dwelling on it any further since it's the past. There are times in everyone's lives where things from their past cause issues down the road for them. Regardless of whether it influences their relationships, acquaintances, families, their minds etc., it has happened to us all, and I'm no exception.

Many of us experience difficulty moving on from past occasions. They can be extremely awful, or unbearable to consider. Choosing not to move on is something we shouldn't do any more, in spite of the fact that, it is easier said than done.

The past is the past. Nobody is perfect, we are prone to make mistakes. In any case, that is okay because we're all human.

What's done is done. Whatever has occurred in your past, you have outdone and overcome it. You are still here, and maybe more grounded than at any other time.

Passing judgment on people based on how they used to be, or for something they did some time back, isn't reasonable. Individuals change after some time. I'm not the same person I was in primary school, or secondary school. I'm not in any way the same individual I was a year prior. Time and circumstances change individuals. Indeed, some of the time it's not to improve things, but you will never realize except if you give individuals the opportunity. It would be a disservice to pass judgment on me based on how I was a couple of years back in secondary school.

There is no benefit in reviving or reliving past occurrences—particularly horrible or negative ones. In some cases individuals can't control what occurs in their lives. Persons respond diversely in a wide range of circumstances. It would be a disgrace to belittle somebody as a result of something they did years ago or how they acted some time back. Persons deserve renewed opportunities and a new beginning. Now this may not be easy but the same open-mindedness you would like to be granted should be extended to another. In the same way you would not want to be judged based on previous actions, you should extend the same courtesy.

I'm not saying this applies for all circumstances, but if you are passing judgment on somebody from what you heard of them or from how they were, that isn't right.

I can't overemphasize that the past is the past. There have been some great memories and some not all that great. Yet, I would prefer not to be neglected as a person in light of the awful incidents which may have taken place throughout my life.

It's damaging to revive or relive terrible memories from the past. It's difficult to relinquish them too. However, the best activity is to embrace the here and now and be cheerful for what is to come.

My past has helped shape me into the individual I am today. Despite the fact that dwelling on tough instances in our lives is normal, and frequently is a hard tendency to break, taking a look at the past as a learning experience as opposed to a difficult time can help give an individual some closure.

The enemy uses our past to cause disarray and confusion in our lives. He is the record manager of the past. He torments us with feelings of disgrace, blame, judgment, and a host of other terrible emotions. He wants to help us to remember things we have done to shield us from feeling meriting God's love and grace. Indeed, even things we may have had no power over he will use to make us feel guilty.

The enemy caused me to remember each terrible thing I had done. Indeed, there were things upon things. He disgraced me and ridiculed my life so much, that guilt prevented me from venturing a foot within a congregation.

In this manner, I placed a barrier between me and God for a couple of months. It happened so often until the point that I had to expel that control from the past. The adversary can use the past to drive a wedge between man and God.

That baggage we carry for a considerable length of time; the oversights, scars, hurt, and betrayal we take it from relationship to relationship, or keep it covered some place where it counts inside. It's time to let it go.

When we take a look at the Bible we see God giving us stories after stories about individuals who were killers, adulterers, liars, criminals, con artists, just individuals that were loaded with chaos and sin. God forgave them as well as utilized them for amazing purposes.

Wouldn't you say there is a reason that a significant number of those accounts are shared all through Scriptures? Don't you think there is a reason that He reveals to us what those wrongdoings were?

He didn't simply say Paul did a few things that we won't discuss, no, Paul killed Christians. The Scripture doesn't state, Peter said a few things that were malicious, no, Peter denied Jesus Christ multiple times.

God discloses to us the depth of these wrongdoings so we can see that there is nothing too unusual or too sinful that the blood of Jesus can't wash clean!

For a few, our mess, later turns into a message God wants us to use for another person going through a similar circumstance. However, we are so burdened with blame and too embarrassed to even consider talking about it.

The savvier I move toward becoming (or a greater method for saying it is "the more established I get"), the more I have figure out how to value that the best things in life are the ones that take work, exposure, punishment, and are once in a while frightening, offers the best reward.

The most profound part about my terrible past is that it presently offers a start to my stunning change; I am a mobile declaration to the affection, generosity, and elegance of Christ.

Also the more I gloat in my shortcoming and praise God for His grace and compassion, the less valuable it progresses toward the adversary. Satan can't torment me with a past I use as a declaration to extol our King!

Being powerless is alarming. Our transgressions might be odd, yet every Christian has a past. Jesus would say, "let him without sin cast the first stone", not one person attempted to carry out "justice." It's the delightful piece of elegance, and the association we should all recognize in our walk together.

In the event that there are bits of your past that you can't give up, possibly it is on the grounds that God is pushing you to transform your chaos into your message.

Everyone has issues and we all have torments. The question however is, how are we going to manage it? Seeing that everyone plays on their past, nothing would be accomplished we would all be trapped. I'm worried about the possibility that is the thing that has happened with most of us. We have allowed our past traumas to cause us present day drama.

Your future has just been resolved. Carry on with your life with confidence in Jesus Christ, and grip to the fact that God provides for the individuals who He considers His own. You don't need to give your present a chance to decide your future.

Let go and let God.

Chapter 8:
Personal Experience

In high school I was verbally and emotionally abused. I developed an angry spirit and became aggressive. So much so that my parents especially my mother became very concerned. With all the abuse I was facing there was no outlet, I wasn't speaking to anyone and so it was all being internalized. I became uncomfortable with living. I was going to church, being involved, playing music and preaching, but I was still not comfortable living.

I remember during this time my five years relationship just ended without a reason. The night it ended I developed a severe headache. I took a pill which I did not know I was allergic to and took an overdose. My mom had to rush me to the hospital and I was admitted for four days. I thought this was rough because going through an emotional abuse and then a break up caused more physical damage than good.

After leaving the hospital I started isolating myself. I would just hide away in my room because when I'm was around people they couldn't tell I was going through anything emotional and that hurt even more. I became a loner; I was suicidal. I could not see any way out, and I felt like a complete failure. It was not a case of wanting death, but more so no longer wanting life—I was just so tired of everything. Being a student at Jamaica College there was the stigma that men don't cry so I buried the feelings and carried on. If you're experiencing suicidal feelings, know that you are not alone!

One of the things that really inspires me is the insight my volunteering gives me. At any time, no matter who you are, or what you have done, there are always people out there who are willing to drop what they are doing to come to your aid. Complete strangers, with no expectation of reward or thanks.

Do not be afraid to reach out and say, "I am feeling like a waste. I am having thoughts of suicide. I need a little help." Things can always get better. No matter how bad they are, tomorrow is a new chance for a better day. And if you know someone who's experiencing suicidal feelings, don't judge them, don't be dismissive, don't laugh, just listen, show empathy, and show respect. If someone is feeling suicidal, what they need is a little love, care, and compassion. You don't need to fix their problems, you just have to support them while they fix themselves or seek assistance.

After recovering from the break up my church organization had a mentorship program. This program was to guide and train potential persons how to teach, moderates and of course preach. Without hesitation, I signed up for it. After the mentorship program I became a Junior Minister in training. During this training I was attending The University of the West Indies.

After the training my aunt who is a minister, visited Jamaica. She allowed one of her colleagues in ministry to pray for my family, my dad, my mom and myself. My sister was not there at the time. The pastor began to prophesy, and he told me God was going to break me, so he can use me. He told me that persons who I think are my friends are going to leave me during this period. The persons that are close to me will not be there when I need them. He told me that God is going to strip me but do not give up for God is only shaping me for what is to come. And I have to go through this alone.

A week after, things started to fall apart. One month after I was suspended for an incident I got involved in. And the enemy just found a way to creep in and started turning my life upside down.

It is said that the church is a place of grace and mercy but I have yet to prove that notion true! Sadly my church is the opposite of what restoration should resemble and reflect, and has not yet attained that status to date. I know this because I have personally felt the hands of church critics and it wasn't the constructive one. I have felt the teeth of church pain, experienced broken heart, and abandonment, dished down judgments, cast aside and long forgotten!

Before my experience of grief and pain in the church, the church in my perspective was a little safe haven; a place where you can run to when the world turns its back on you; a place where when you feel like there is no hope, you can receive hope, a place where if persons are merciless toward you, you will be shown mercy. The church in my eyes was the symbol of who Jesus was and is, but that held notion was just in my mind; and was only but an imagination.

I just got appointed as a Junior Minister and got elected to be a part of the Caribbean Conference of Seventh-Day Christians' Executive board. And just as quickly, I got suspended as a Junior Minister got kicked off the executive board and all the offices I held in my local church. I was stripped of all these offices. This was the most embarrassing moment of my life.

Even though I was suspended, I was still attending church. I didn't rebel, I was just staying to myself. Until the issue of whether or not I should play musical instruments arose. The majority decided I should not play. I was taken aback by the response because being a musician wasn't an office. Musicians came from outside and played at church regardless of them being saved or unsaved. Taking all these blows I still continued to attend church facing one dilemma after the other. My best friend got suspended the same time I did because she got pregnant outside of marriage and a rumor began to circulate that I was the father.

Persons I thought would be there, weren't. Close friends left me hanging, close relatives condemned me, persons I thought I could lean on at church in my rough times gave up on me. But I was reminded that Elijah had to face Baal and his prophets alone on Mount Carmel, so I just held the fort.

Suspension affected me psychologically, emotionally, physically, spiritually and mentally. Whilst it was an action that caused me to be suspended, it robbed me of my integrity and trust especially because I was assigned to a position that seeks to uphold loyalty.

The area that was affected first was my mental capacity. This was so because I began to think about the issues and try to work in my head where did I go wrong and at times blamed myself.

Thoughts like, what caused me to do that? People are going to see me as a bad person and I feel like killing myself as I am no longer worthy to live.

The spiritual side of my life is critical to my personal growth and development. We are physical beings and those around us can see the ripple effects that are associated with this aspect of life. On the other hand, spirituality is deep and it helps one to be rooted and grounded in a belief that is geared towards hope for a better day and even greater a better life.

When the suspension was given, after a while it caused me to think about the existence of

God. For most cases, the devil was blamed and what was committed became the center of attention. It erased most if not all the good that I was known for and the negative was the light for all to see.

I was asked the question by a mature church member at my local church, "What are you doing here?" With the facial expression of being unwanted. Feeling this way, one week, I decided not to go to church but to stay at home. I was sleeping in the afternoon and when I woke up I was attacked by a demon. I was in a powerless state. I started doing things I had no control over. I was conscious of what I was doing but had no control. I started doing things that a psychiatric person would do. I went to the hospital and the doctor wanted to send me to a psychiatric ward to be admitted. I didn't go!

I felt like I was being stripped of my pride, dignity, mercy, grace, soul, freedom and my entire life. My previously held beliefs about what the church should epitomize was shattered like a broken glass being hit by an idle stone. It was at that very moment I gave up on church. I lost all hope in the one place that I thought hope was abounding.

I told myself that never again am I going back there, and I didn't. I started attending church less frequently, I didn't feel comfortable. I could not worship because everywhere I looked I could see the eyes staring at me, and the expressions on their faces were never the forgiving look. It was never the look that said I am here for you, you have our support and love. I could tell what they were thinking, call it my mind, but just the thought of them being judgmental made me sick.

I was withdrawn from fellowship, I could not even participate in the worship because even the songs, testimonies and words spoken felt like a stone was being thrown at me. I could not function in that environment because I was literally melting in pain and shame, and the sad part about it was that nobody saw that! How I longed to be held, hugged and accepted without being judged. I longed for that welcoming smile and that open arm of help and restitution.

At one point, I started seeing the demon that was attacking me. I saw the demon that wanted me to go insane enter my room on more than one occasion. Even though I was weak spiritually the demon could not overpower me. When the first demon could not achieve what he came to achieve, he came back stronger than before. For one month I was seeing demons. I saw the demon who came and made me dumb. I was dumb for one week; I saw the demon that came to take my life, but they can't kill what God has anointed to live.

At one point, I almost got locked up by the police. Persons, including relatives, use this to their advantage to tell lies to say I did things I didn't do because as stated before I was conscious of what I was doing but had no control. I could tell what I did but couldn't explain how it happened.

During this time I was still going to school. My father was so afraid to even send me. When I finally hit rock bottom, my deliverance came. One day my mother called three persons to come to the house and they prayed. At this point I was so far from God, I thought I could not find my way back. It was through these experiences I found out that brokenness brings breakthrough.

Chapter 9:
Brokenness Brings
Breakthrough

believe in this time and in this season, God is going to elevate individuals to their next dimension of power.

There will be an incredible need in the not so distant future for faithful members in the body of Christ. God wants us to know and understand not just how to get through to the next dimension, but likewise to support the expansion He gives. It is one thing to get a push forward, but it's something else to keep it.

God is bringing individuals into a higher realm of power, yet we should know this won't come without a battle. Before David could venture into his fate and into the higher dimension of power, he needed to confront Goliath. The expansion and advancement were not going to come without a battle.

Before you venture into the next level God has for you, you should confront your Goliath head-on and bring it down. Your next level won't come without a battle. Understand this about your monster: It will address you; it will attempt, as far as possible to prevent you from having what is yours in God. It will address you with words like, "Who do you think you are? You think God has a plan for you? Do you think God will ever utilize you?" The words you hear will come in connection to the territory of fight you are confronting. "Do you think you will be free? Do you think things will change? Things are never going to change. You are going to prop up around this mountain. You are nothing. Simply surrender and quit!"

Blessing without testing isn't supportable. God wouldn't like to simply give us a temporary blessing or a skimming push forward. He wants us to almost certainly support it. The support factor is vital in this hour. We should battle for an increase and continue it.

Before breakthrough you have to walk through a position of brokenness. You have to battle with your Goliath and triumph over it before the blessing is discharged to show in a more noticeable share of power. God blessed what was disappointment in David's life. God wants to bless what's disappointing you in your life.

David couldn't win the fight in Saul's protective gear. It hadn't been tried in his life. David wrestled the lion and the bear. He had utilized his sling and stone out in the wild.

Progression will leave your testings and fights. Littler fights will make you apt in winning bigger ones. Rejoice, in light of the fact that the zones of your trials are going to end up in the territories of your most prominent blessing. The very assignments the enemy had against your life are going to be pivoted against him. God will discharge the most profound blessing and greatness in those areas where you have had the most profound dimension of fighting and battling.

As Isaac was going into his territory of legacy in Genesis 26, we see that he began in a position of infertility. As he planted and sowed seed in that land, he turned out to be extremely prosperous and productive. God quickened his yield and around the same time, he harvested a hundredfold. Be that as it may, God still had more increment for him.

The Philistines envied him and started to cover the wells of Abraham. With the end goal for Isaac to get through to a larger amount of productivity in his legacy, he needed to battle with the Philistines. He therefore started to dig wells, the first was called Esek, which means conflict. The following well was called Sitnah, which means hatred. The third well was called Rehoboth, which means room. As Isaac drove forward and suffered, God prepared for him to be productive in the land. The key for Isaac's breakthrough was continuance.

As we suffer through a position of dispute, God will account for us and cause us to be productive in our property of legacy. Increase and expansion are coming, however not without a battle. So to win this fight, we might suffer as far as possible for a while.

We are in a period where many are confronting their Goliaths. They are in a period of profound weight and obstruction, and what they do in this fight will decide their next season. It is possible that they will continue what God has given them and experience an expansion or lose what has been depended to them.

God wants us to understand the greatness of brokenness. There is a major contrast between common suffering and genuine suffering, between common brokenness and faithful brokenness. Give me a chance to demonstrate to you an extraordinary precedent.

Saul's heart had turned out to be loaded with resentment, frailty, envy, abhor, murder, resistance and the dread of man. At the point when Saul's transgression had gone up against God, he recognized it. We see this in 1 Samuel 15:30, where he unmistakably says, "I have trespassed." But quickly following this announcement, he says, "Yet please respect me before the older folks, and before Israel." Saul was increasingly worried about his dishonor before the general population than he was in with lamenting God and losing the Holy Spirit. He had a shameless distress.

At that point there was David. David was not perfect. He gave in to some awful sins, including murder and adultery. Yet, the Bible still considers him a man after God's own heart. Why? It was not a direct result of his flawlessness but rather in light of the understanding of his authentic distress and apology. David's primary concern was not his notoriety. In Psalm 51, we see David's heart when he shouts out for God not to take His Holy Spirit from him. David's primary concern was lamenting the core of God and losing the Holy Spirit. This was the contrast between David and Saul's heart. One thought about dishonor and respect before man. The other thought about God's heart and closeness.

Saul lost his mantle and blessing because in light of the fact that his heart became hardened, and he needed authentic misery. In spite of the fact that David still had consequences for his wrongdoing, the reason he had the capacity to support his mantle and blessing was a direct result of the understanding of his dimension of brokenness and faithful pain.

We should have the core of David if we want to see and keep the expansion and blessings God has for us. We should think most about God's heart and have a sacred, faithful brokenness before the Lord.

The keys to moving higher will be our capacity to persevere through and our dimension of genuine authentic brokenness over what laments the core of God. As we face and bring down our Goliaths, we will be situated before the Lord for increment, increase and productivity. Out of obvious brokenness will rise a blessing that will get extraordinary in the lives of God's children.

Chapter 10:
My Restoration

I woke up one night crying so hard because I couldn't tolerate it any longer. The torment, hurt and how harmed I was, was unbearable to the point that I believed I was just a single affliction, and God was rejecting me. At that point I heard God obviously in my soul saying, "My child, I will wipe every one of your tears and say thanks to me since I am preparing you for what is to come."

I immediately wiped my tears, stooped down and spilled out my heart to God, not for realizing what I ought to be grateful for but rather with a genuine heart, since I knew the plans He had for me are great, greater than my plans. I came up from my petition feeling so refreshed, encouraged and energized. That is all that made a difference.

At this point, I remembered I started playing "don't count me out" by Jermaine Edwards. To this day I can relate to the entire song which says:

In my life I had so many low seasons,
A lot of failures without reason,
Many people try so many times to tear me down,
Never prayed, I tried to pick me up off the ground.
They said I wasn't going to make it very far,
Look in my life and I got so many scars,
It wasn't easy but I really worked hard,
Always having Father God in my heart.
Don't count me out yet I'm still running,
Fall down but I got up fighting,
My eyes are on God's Kingdom always,
But I won't stop until I finish this race.
I know I'm not where I'm supposed to be,
But I'm trying to be the man God wants me to be,
Don't let nobody distract me from my dreams,
Even if my friends turn my enemies.
Honestly sometimes I feel so lonely.
And I wonder if God is walking with me,

I see one set of footprints in the sand,
It was God always caring me.
Don't count me out yet I'm still running,
Fall down but I got up fighting,
My eyes are on God's Kingdom always,
And I won't stop until I finish this race.

—Jermaine Edwards

After coming off suspension I was called to many meetings both within the organization and outside of it. In one of the meetings to which my parents had accompanied me, I remember how I was called all sort of derogative names. Negative things were said about me and like Jesus, as the lamb before the slaughter I refrained from saying anything. It was almost as if I couldn't speak to be honest even if I wanted to. I just could only witness as a series of events of propaganda were thrown before me regarding tales about my life. I was literally just standing there watching as someone laid out every past mistake, fiction story and astounding accusations about me.

After the meeting my dad told me his entire heart moved, he felt the pain and hurt I was going through. Looking back, I do not know if it was because of the extremity of the situation that rendered us silent or if the hurt closed off all other reactions but I do know that in those moments we said little or nothing.

I was on the other side while my accusers seemingly had the upper hand in the situation. They spoke first, changed subjects and seemingly were more convicted than me. A part of me was weakened when my past that I was redeemed of was brought to the forefront of the conflict to make me appear as the villain even more. I felt I was losing the battle and all I wanted in that moment was to disappear.

Despite my feelings of defeat whilst leaving the meeting, I remember hearing the voice of God whisper to me and two scriptures were imprinted upon my heart.

"He knows the way that I take and when He hath tried me I shall come forth as gold" (Job 23:10).

Beloved, think it not strange concerning the fiery trial which is to try you, as though some strange thing happened unto you: But rejoice, inasmuch as ye are partakers of Christ's sufferings; that, when his glory shall be revealed, ye may be glad also with exceeding joy (1st Peter 4:12-13).

In spite of my feelings of neglect and betrayal I still felt the urge to continue, I was still motivated by God to try. In that same week I had a sermon to preach at one of the churches in the organization. I remember it was youth month and the theme was 'Time for a new beginning '. With moments of praying and seeking the Lord I decided to preach from Job 42:10. The Lord spoke throughout the congregation that day not only to them, but to me as well. As I ministered I could feel it from the depths of my soul that I would overcome.

Following the revelation of my impending restoration I began to encourage myself through prayer and fasting and by listening to music.

These are some of the songs I listened to and I would encourage you to listen to these songs as well:

1. This too shall pass by Yolanda Adams
2. The best in me by Marvin Sapp
3. Don't worry by Rev FC Barnes
4. I go to the rock by Whitney Houston
5. I must tell Jesus by Grace Thrillers

Lyrically and spiritually these songs stood out and motivated me to keep holding on. They reminded me of God's promises and I believed them.

I realized that as the scriptures say "when I am weak therefore I am strong." A new hunger began to form in my system that had me craving for more of the Word and that's where I really began to understand and meditate on the word of God. God started to reveal Himself through His words and that's where I found comfort in Psalm 30:5: "For his anger endureth but a moment; in His favour is life: weeping may endure for a night, but joy cometh in the morning." I also found comfort in Psalm 126:5: "they that sow in tears shall reap in joy."

In Psalm 3:1-3, I found refuge "Lord, how are they increased that trouble me! Many are they that rise up against me. Many there be which say of my soul, there is no help for him in God. But thou, O Lord, art a shield for me; my glory, and the lifter up of mine head."

I rest on God's promises in Isaiah 43:18-19, which declares "Remember ye not the former things, neither consider the things of old. Behold, I will do a new thing; now it shall spring forth; shall ye not know it? I will even make a way in the wilderness, and rivers in the desert."

These scriptures not only stood out to me and helped me in the process of rebuilding my strength but they helped me to feel the depth that the word of God carried even tenfold.

I stopped venting and started praying, because what I needed was strength not sympathy. I found myself in a period where in the wee hours of the mornings, sometime as early as 3 a.m, I would get up and fall on my knees and to talk to God. And this wasn't something I had usually done so often! I needed strength and so I prayed for just that!

One Sabbath evening I was coming from church my cousin and I were walking and she started singing "people see one wrong but Jah Jah see one right, people see darkness but Jah Jah see sunlight." This song touched me. I asked her where she got the song she said she heard it on the radio. I went home and search for the song and the song was speaking to the situation I went through.

This song was written by Jah-Lil in Jamaican Creole. The words of the song are:

People see one wrong, Jah Jah see one right
yeh
People see darkness, Jah Jah see sunlight
Them just a susu susu susu so
And when you buck your toe them will say
"you bugger you"
Long time you consistent them never feature
you,
But as soon as you fall ah so them picture
you, oh
I rather people write me off than Jah Jah
fight me off
Or people fight me off then Jah Jah write me
off
I rather people write me off than Jah Jah
fight me off
So gwaan fight it, fight me, Jah Jah like me
People see one wrong, Jah Jah see one right
People see darkness, yeah yeah, Jah Jah see
sunlight
When they say I'm doing right you're by my
side
But when you feel I'm doing wrong you run
go and hide
In the presence of the almighty I will abide
cause if you try to live for people you slip
and slide

You got a plank in your eye
So why you inspecting me oww
And you're almost blind
Let Jah jah see the speck in me
Is like you study the law thing
You keep on judging me, while Jesus set me
    free

—Jah-Lil

Eventually God even sent some awesome persons in my life to help me during my period of restoration. Persons who helped me to understand the concept of life. I was shown that when situations come by me, I could decide how to move forward as I was not to be defined by my situations or circumstances. I was shown that decisions we make as well impact outcomes and that God is still watching with His hand outstretched for us to take. I came to understand that most definitely without challenges there would be no victory, that to grow you needed to fall at one point! I learnt that seasons of loneliness could be used as the time we take to know God.

Earth has no sorrows that heaven cannot heal. If you can have it, God can heal it, If there's a void, God can fill it.

Chapter 11:
God Will Restore You

You might be going through a tough time, struggling to keep your head above water, you're smiling just to keep from crying, you're going to church but there is still aches and pain in your body. You're doing the best you can, but you take one step forward and two steps backwards. You're trying but things don't seem to be working out the way you want it to work out. You thought you would be at a different place or a different season in your life, and it looks like you've been praying and calling on the Lord and reading your bible, doing your morning devotions and listening to the word of God. You're doing everything right, but you're still suffering. Anybody can be a Christian and sing songs when the sun is shining. It doesn't take much faith to give God glory when all your bills are paid.

It is so easy to worship God when things are going well in your life. However, it is also equally important to give God thanks when things aren't going the way you want. For instance, you should still continue to praise him even in sickness, in depression, when your children break your heart, and even when you are experiencing hardships. During your time of hardships, you have to continue to have faith and lean on the belief that God is a very present help in time of trouble.

This book is written to encourage someone who has experienced brokenness in the form of: a broken heart, a broken body, a broken family, a broken marriage and perhaps even a broken relationship. Where are the persons who are believing that God is who He said He is? And where are the persons who are believing that God will do what He says He will do? Often we think the breaking disqualifies us from the call of God, but I personally have discovered that it's the breaking that often qualifies us to God's calling.

I have to let you know that in the midst of your test there will be a testimony. After you have gone through the process, you will be able to testify to somebody that God is able to deliver you and bring you out of every circumstance. I want you to know whatever the battle is, God has given you power. He has given you authority and dominion over all the works of the devil. So, you are not defeated but you have got the victory, you're above and not beneath. You're the head and not the tail. You're blessed in the city, and you are blessed in the field. It doesn't matter what you are going through; you are still blessed. Even though sometimes the enemy looks like he has the upper hand, but the word of God declares that "all things work together for good" (Romans 8:28)

Who or what will separate you from the love of God? You are going to go through tribulations. Nobody told you that the road would be easy, but I don't believe he has brought you this far to leave you. You must understand that even though you must go through tribulations and you must go through perils you must understand that all of this is working for your good. Someway, somehow, something good is going to come out of what you are going through. You must stop complaining about it and recognize that He's going to get the glory from what you are going through. The trying of your faith is more precious than gold.

There are all kinds of different ways to break. You can break physically, you can break mentally, you can break your heart, you can break your spirit and none of those are fun. All of those are going to leave a mark. But the mark that they leave can be the mark of victory, or it can be the mark of defeat. When I'm broken, I relish it. That's what I'm going to do, because if I am broken then I just found my limitations. Until I know what my limitations are, how can I push it? How can I get better? Once I feel it, once I see where I was broken then I can attack that weakness. I can fill in that gap. If you break it means. It's time to fortify your will to make it stronger. Every time you break and in every way that you break, it's a chance for you to give up and for you to fall apart. But there's also opportunity. There's opportunity to get stronger, smarter, tougher, more stable and re-silient to get better.

No matter where you are in life, no matter how low you have sunk no matter how bleak your situation looks, this is not the end. This is not the end of your story. This is not the final chapter of your life. I know it may be hard right now but just hang in there. Stick it out. Stay for a little while. You will find that this tough moment will pass and if you are committed to using this pain to build your character, finding a greater meaning for the pain, you will find that in time you can turn your life around and help others going through the same struggles.

The world right now is in the middle of a mental health crisis. It's estimated almost half the population suffers from depression at some stage throughout their life. Rather than join the que, it's important that we learn why we get down and how we can change it. Believe it or not, we create our own negative feelings and we can also ensure that we turn our lives around and be a positive change for others.

The reason anyone gets depressed always comes down to the consistent thoughts we think and the consistent beliefs we hold. Read that again; the reason anyone gets depressed always comes down to the thoughts we think and the beliefs we hold. The point here is that anyone who is depressed is so because there is an external factor that didn't materialize in their life. They have lost something outside of their control or don't have something that is out of their control. In school we are taught how to get a job, but no one teaches us how to live in a state of happiness. No one teaches us how important our conscious and unconscious thoughts and associations are.

Is our happiness not worth more than a job? Yes, it is. Before you say happiness won't pay my bills, happiness will pay your bills. You will be 10 times more energized, focused and take positive actions in your life, when you first choose to develop yourself as a priority and then get to the stuff of the world.

You must value yourself enough to take the time every single day to work on you, to engage in something that will ensure you are a positive influence on the world. This of course doesn't mean life will be perfect, the same life challenges will show up. But if your mind is strong, if your mind is at ease, your reaction to the challenging times will be very different. Your reaction will be 'how can I make this work? Not "why is this happening to me?" And then others will look to you not with pity but with hope because your strength will become their hope, their strength. You really can be that powerful. You can leave the pain behind and focus on how you will react next. How you will react positively. All you need to do to get your mind in a positive place is to read. Take steps to ensure you will be in a better position next time.

Whatever pain you are suffering from, how you can ensure it won't show again? Take little steps and soon you will be at the top of the staircase. Don't give up. You are worthy. You are more than worthy. You deserve to experience how great life can be and you owe it to the world to be that positive change for others. Inspire others who will look to you and say he did it. She did it, and I can do it too.

Trust God. Two single syllable words that you have heard forever but you will discover as time passes how difficult they are to obey. Trust God. Of course I have no way of knowing what the future holds for you. You may lose your home in a fire, you may lose your spouse to an early disease, detected but not cured. You may lose your dreams, your hopes. You may lose your relationship that you have cultivated over the years. All losses are painful. There will always be unanswered questions. Why didn't my loved one make it? Why am I not getting better? Why did this person leave?

Some things are not going to make sense, but God wouldn't have allowed it if He wasn't going to bring good out of it. You may not see it at the time, but God knows what He is doing. He has your best interest at heart it's not random, it's a part of his plan. Trust in the Lord with all your heart and lean not to your own undertaking. In all your ways acknowledge Him and He will make your paths straight. All your heart, all your ways, trust, trust.

But what about when things aren't going our way. Our prayers aren't being answered, the problem isn't turning around, and we're not seeing favor. Too often we get discouraged and think, *God, why aren't you doing something?* You can see I'm being mistreated. My health isn't good I worked hard but I didn't get the promotion. We think when it changes we will be happy. When I meet the right person, when my health improves, when we have this baby, then we will have a good attitude. That's conditional trust. God if you meet my demands if you answer my prayers the way I want on my timetable, then I'll be my best.

The problem with conditional trust is there will always be things we don't understand. Something that is not happening fast enough, it didn't work out the way we want it. If I would have had conditional trust I would have gotten up, said "bitter God why didn't you answer my prayers?" The truth is God did answer my prayers. It just wasn't the way I wanted. Are you mature enough to accept God's answers even though they're not what you were hoping for? God is a sovereign God. We're not going to understand everything that happens.

Faith is trusting God when life doesn't make sense. God doesn't take us in a straight line. There will be twists and turns, the disappointments, the losses, the bad breaks. They are all a part of his plan. But if you have conditional trust, you'll get discouraged and think why this is happening. I'm going the wrong way. But God is still directing your steps. Trust him when you don't understand. Trust Him even when it feels like you're going the wrong direction. Living worried, frustrated and disappointed takes our passion. It steals our joy and it can keep us from seeing God's favor.

Sometimes the closed doors, the disappointments, they are simply a test. God wants to see if we will trust him when we don't understand it. When life doesn't make sense. We must show him that we don't have to have the house to be happy. If we don't have the baby, we're not going to live bitter and sour. You are believing for your health to improve. But when you can say if it doesn't get better God I'm still going to honor you. I'm still going to be my best.

Are you living frustrated because your prayers aren't being answered the way you want? Take the pressure off. God is in control. He knows what's best for you. You're not always going to understand it, if you did it wouldn't take any faith. I'm asking you to trust him unconditionally. If you'll do this, I believe and declare God is going to work out his plan for your life. He is going to open the right doors, bring the right people, turn negative situations around and take you to the fullness of your destiny.

Most of this generation quits the second they get talked to... 'You did this wrong', or 'you did this wrong' or they get yelled at. It's so easy to be great nowadays, because everybody else is, most people are weak. This is a softened generation. So, if you have any mental toughness, any ability, if you have any fraction of self-discipline... the ability to not want to do it, but still do it... If you can get through to doing things that you hate to do, on the other side is greatness. What is it with our society? We are creating weak individuals. Individuals that can't handle anything going wrong in their lives. As soon as something goes wrong... they are given a prescription. Not to fix the problem, to mask the problem.

How about giving strategies to strengthen the mind? How about saying, ok, you've allowed your life to get to this point... now take responsibility... and dive deep into personal development. Learn why you feel this way—not because of the event—the scientific facts about why you feel the way you do, and what you can do to strengthen it.

The moment they are criticized—rather than take any of it on board, rather than prove any of those people wrong—they give up, they attempt to defend the criticism with useless talk, but never with definitive action. The moment they are challenged, they crumble. The moment things get hard they declare defeat "it must not be for me"... "It was their fault, if they didn't do this or treat me like this or say this" then I would have made it. No. You're just soft. You're weak. Tell yourself the truth. Because until you do that until you look in the mirror and acknowledge that YOU are the problem, you'll never be able to grow into the person that can achieve all those things you want. You are the problem, the only problem. Your mindset is the problem. Your attitude is the problem. It is no one else's fault! It's yours! If you want the good news: you are also the solution. You and only you.

If you have character—that statement will change your life, if you have no character you'll remain an average, complaining hater, like most other people. You are your only problem and you are the only solution. Sure, big things happen. Tragic loss, things which no one would deserve. I'm not talking about those things, I'm talking about the people who are one job loss away from a break down. One relationship break up away from depression. One argument ruins their entire week. Come on people... this is not how to live. Even with the big stuff—if you have perspective—if you know who you are... if you really, really appreciate everything you do have and believe everything is as it should be, all those big things can be handled much better. Knowing your loved one would want you to be happy and move on.

Knowing that living in pain and holding on to resentment—is letting that person who did you wrong win—but letting go and living your life, loving your life—that is you saying I won! That is, you are saying I will not allow you to own any piece of my mind and spirit. That is true courage and mental strength. And I'm not saying avoid pain. Pain, suffering, failures—they are all a part of every single person's life. There are varying levels of pain for sure, some suffer more than others, but we all suffer at some level. Some choose, consciously or unconsciously, to live in that pain, and some decide to move on. You deserve to move on.

Mental strength comes from those struggles, it is formed from pain, it is increased when you refuse to give up at times when most others would. It grows when you keep going when things seem impossible. It grows when you push one more time past what you thought was your limit. It grows with consistency! That is mental strength! Excuses are for weak individuals. Individuals who have no heart. Take responsibility for where you are now, and commit to do something, anything, whatever it takes to make sure your future is better. You have the choice. You can make excuses and stay where you are or get worse. Or, you can take responsibility, act, and get where you need to go, where you DESERVE to go.

What do you choose? Stop dancing around the truth by finding the right words so I don't hurt you because you have thin skin. No. Tighten up people. It's ok trust me. It's ok. You might be called *nigger* one day. It's ok. You might be called some Jewish word or some faggot or gay word, it's ok. Let them call you that. What are you going to do now, they don't own your life. How are you going to control that now? How are you going to flip it upside down and say "roger that?" Now I'm going to harness this and you'll read about me years from now. How? That's the question. How? Thicken your skin. Become more a human being. Don't be afraid of the reflection in the mirror because that's all you can be afraid of. Once you over-come the reflection in the mirror, you've done it.

We can all probably recall a situation that has gone from bad to worse. I'm not talking about in your neighbor's life. I'm not talking about in one of your cousin's lives. I'm talking about in your life. We've all had a time in our life where it was bad and we thought it couldn't get any worse but we found ourselves a few minutes or a few moments or a few days after our bad situation in finding out that our situation has even gotten worse, and just when we thought we had ourselves together, it got even worse than we thought it would ever get.

Sometimes we can see the trouble coming. Sometimes we'll be in a situation and we will see that the situation is about to get worse but there are times when it appears that there are sunny days in our forecast. It seemed as if all the bad weather is behind us but out of nowhere storm clouds begin to roll. And I wonder is there anyone here other than me who at one time in your life you thought you had it together and all of a sudden storms showed up? Well maybe you may be the exemplary one to the rule and you may say I never had any bad days in my life, but I need to drop this in your email account...

If it has not rained in your life all of your days have been good; if you never had to struggle, if you never had to cry, if you never had to look like you were down to your last, keep on living. Job said man born of a woman is of a few days and full of trouble. I'm trying to tell you today that sooner or later trouble is going to come, don't wait until trouble shows up to figure out a way out.

How many of you look like you're happy but, on the inside, tears are rolling down your face. You came in and spoke to everybody this morning, but you really wanted to just fall on your knees because you've been beat up. All week long some of you, your life may be like mine shattered into a thousand pieces. Just because your life is shattered that does not mean it's time for you to drown. Just because you're going through something, just because the odds may look like they're not in your favor does not mean it's time for you to throw in the towel.

God can restore you by bringing *long-haul gain* from temporary misfortune. The impact of these trials throughout your life will be so that

"The testing of your faith which may result in praise and honor and admiration at the revelation of Jesus Christ" (1 Peter 1:7).

The praise, honor, and admiration go to Christ since His power and supremacy protected you and kept you through the hardest time of your life. And God is saying I will restore you.

About the Author

Artnel Simon Jr. is a teacher/facilitator at the College of Business, Education, Science and Technology where he is teaching CSEC chemistry and biology.

He attended the University of the West Indies, Mona, where he studied Political Leadership, Strategy and Management and minored in Public Policy Management. At the University of the West Indies, he had the opportunity to sit on the Portmore Municipal Council as a Junior Health Officer. He was the Vice President of the Governance Society UWI, Mona (2016-2017). He also served as the Director of Clubs and Societies and Associations (2017-2018).

He is a young man who is called for such a time as this. He is an appointed Junior Minister who has been preaching for the last 16 years, from when he was eight years old. As a Junior Minister, he has been assigned to all churches in the Caribbean Conference of Seventh-Day Christians. One of his favorite Bible verses is Zechariah 4:6, "So he answered and said to me: "this is the word of the Lord to Zerubbabel: not by might nor by power, but by My Spirit," says the Lord.

His dream is to become a political advisor/consultant and also a theologian.

Contact the author to speak at your next event: brokentoberestored7@gmail.com